The Gift of
Renewal

Best wishes.

[signature]

The Gift of
Renewal

By
CHARLES E. "GUS" WHALEN, JR.
WITH PHILLIP ROB BELLURY

FOREWORD BY EDWARD C. EMMA
PRESIDENT AND COO
JOCKEY INTERNATIONAL, INC.

THE WARREN FEATHERBONE FOUNDATION

The Gift of Renewal

Published by The Warren Featherbone Foundation
999 Chestnut Street SE, Gainesville, GA 30501-6906
Copyright © 2003 Charles E. "Gus" Whalen, Jr.

Printing: Matthews Printing
Gainesville, GA, USA.

Binding: BindTech
Nashville, TN, USA.

Book design and production
by Shock Design, Inc.
shockdesign@mindspring.com

Billy Howard Photography © 2003 — pages
12-13, 16, 19, 24, 32, 37-38, 43, 68, 71, 79, 92

Travis Massey © 2000— author photo on jacket flap

LC# 2003102350

ISBN# 0-9655107-3-5

5 4 3 2 1   03 04 05 06 07

FIRST EDITION

Contents

Dedication

This book is dedicated to my wife Nell who has always seen the best in me and made sure I found it too.

Nell is also my editor. After reading the first manuscript of The Gift of Renewal, *she offered, "I'm not sure, but there may be a book in there somewhere." Then we got to work as we have for 36 years. That's where love lives – in the "work" of life. Many others joined us in the process, but it started with Nell. This book and renewal in my life would not have been possible without her.*

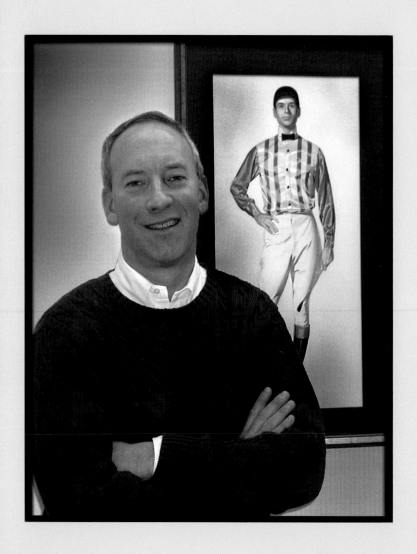

Edward C. Emma

Foreword

I SAT IN THE DARK HOSPITAL ROOM BESIDE MY YOUNGER BROTHER DAN'S BED – as he gently breathed life into the silence – and wondered what I could possibly add to Gus' inspiring book about renewal. As I paged through the manuscript, it became apparent that the answer lay right beside me. For two weeks, my entire family prayed incessantly for just one thing – renewal; renewal for Dan's mind, body, and most importantly, spirit, without which there could be no hope of fully overcoming the pernicious aftermath of his aneurysm and stroke. Only a few days before, the doctor had informed me that they nearly lost Dan once or twice during the prior weekend. Now he lay beside me, immobilized on his right side, his speech slurred and halting when he could muster the energy to speak, and with some loss of vision. I was devastated.

I thought back to the frantic initial days in neural ICU, recalling the doctor's words that "Dan was a fighter." Those were words of hope, holding within them the promise of renewal for which I so desperately desired. I believe that hope is the spiritual food that fuels the renewal process much as a seed depends upon the sunshine to achieve its destiny of renewing the earth.

How else can one explain why patients with the attributes of hope and faith achieve restored health faster than those not so inclined? I prayed for the words or actions that would actuate my brother's physical and spiritual renewal and, in so doing, renew my own. One and a half weeks later they came.

As I sat in on one of Dan's physical therapy sessions with his wife, Jennifer, and their three small children, I watched the extremely challenging exercise of trying to coax sensation and movement from Dan's right arm. As the therapist placed the arm in an upright position, she asked him if he could hold up his forearm on his own. Though his hand slipped downward, his forearm remained vertical for several seconds. I uttered an unrestrained "Yes." Then she clasped his hand and asked him to push back on her arm. We witnessed a tiny but perceptible amount of resistance against her pressure – another unrestrained "Yes." I was ecstatic. The sensations of feeling and movement, though nascent, were now undeniably in renewal.

Several days later, I sat in on a review of Dan's condition, arranged and attended by the entire team overseeing his care. There I learned that their objective was to have Dan return home in three weeks as an outpatient. I was incredulous and eager, with Jennifer, to tell him the news. As he heard the words, his eyes almost extended out of his sockets. Still slurring, he blurted out, "You're kidding! I can't believe it. I've got to keep remembering this." It was as if the weight of the world had fallen from his shoulders. He had lost hope and now, for the first time since the accident, it had returned.

Though many long, difficult and even risky days undoubtedly lie ahead, the renewal process has clearly begun, and with it a new appreciation on my part for the almost mystical relationship between renewal and personal human contact that Gus so powerfully captures in this book.

Gus and I share much in common, both being associated with companies over one hundred years old. In these pages, Gus demonstrates that companies, too, need to renew themselves if they are to survive and remain vibrant in a dynamic global marketplace. But this shouldn't surprise anyone. Companies are all about people and only renewed people can bring about renewed companies. I would encourage readers to find their own story of renewal in this delightful and timely book.

EDWARD C. EMMA
PRESIDENT AND CHIEF OPERATING OFFICER
JOCKEY INTERNATIONAL, INC.

STAR GALAXY 4

Chapter One

> *"In living systems, the issue is not
> control, but dynamic connectedness."*
> ERICH JANTSCH, SYSTEMS SCIENTIST

THE SHAPE OF
THINGS TO COME

AS A CHILD, I LOVED TO BUILD MODEL AIRPLANES. I would spend hours bending over tiny wood and plastic parts, glue, paint and directions. When the model was completed, I would put it on a shelf and admire it. It was finished. To my eyes, it was perfect.

We often think of our lives, our families, and our organizations in the same way. We want to build these structures and then stand back to admire them. We want them to stay the way we have sculptured them and painted them. But, of course, they don't. Why? Because they are living systems...and the natural state of living systems is dynamic. What will eventually happen to my model airplane? It will gather dust and, over time, fall to pieces. What will happen to living systems over time? According to chemists, biologists, physicists, and other scientists, a living system will react to a changing environment first with chaos, then with a reordering of its structure that leads to survival. Erich Jantsch, a systems scientist, says that "a living system is a never-resting structure that constantly seeks its own self-renewal." It will change if it has to, to preserve itself.

So we should not be surprised that life often seems chaotic and out of control. I believe it is out of **our** control…**but it is not out of control.** That is a somewhat disquieting thought in that I've always liked the idea (illusion) that I am in control in absolute terms. The good news and reality is that I am not. You're not either. We have responsibilities and commitments to fulfill, but the outcomes are most often not within our power to control. We don't have to carry that weight. Thank God!

Science often teaches us how to look at life and relationships. Sir Isaac Newton formulated and published his three *principles of motion* in 1687 and ushered in a new way of thinking about our world. Newtonian science told us that the forces of life are like the inner workings of a big clock...tightly controlled, predetermined and organized...excluding chaos from the equation altogether. He felt that the goal of science was to uncover all the laws one by one until we know all there is to know.

Today, new science challenges Newtonian thinking. It suggests that there is a consistent relationship between order and chaos. The "chaos theory," developed in the 1960s from the science of meteorology, says that life consists of a vast series of interdependent networks and that what appear to be random occurrences are actually operating within a system of natural laws. It goes on to say that what we can't predict, and may never be able to, are the millions of tiny variables that affect the outcome. These tiny variables are there during times of chaos and change in our lives; life is "predictably unpredictable." Chaos, however, even when uncomfortable, is usually the forerunner of progress and thus a great creative force.

Margaret J. Wheatly has written a superb book entitled *Leadership and the New Science.* In her discussion of the chaos theory she states:

"A system can descend into chaos and unpredictability, yet within that state of chaos the system is held within boundaries that are well-ordered and predictable. Without the partnering of these two great forces, no change or progress is possible. Chaos is necessary to new creative ordering."

An example of new creative ordering in nature is the formation of thunderstorms. As a pilot, I know to expect them

on hot summer afternoons. Moist air is heated by the sun and rises. As the water vapor rises further into the atmosphere, anvil-shaped cumulus clouds form. Then the mass explodes with thunder, lightning and life-giving rain. If we were inside the storm as it was being formed, those occurrences of vapor condensation probably would appear to be chaotic and random. Once we have the perspective of being outside the storm, the shape is more easily seen as well-ordered and predictable. The storm is necessary for the reordering of the atmosphere and the sustenance of life.

What does this say to organizations and people who lead them? Once again, Margaret Wheatly: "No longer the caretakers of control, we become the grand disturbers. We stir things up and roil the pot, looking always to provoke, even to disrupt, until things finally become so confusing that the system must reorganize itself into new forms and behaviors. If we accept this challenge to be equilibrium busters, if we begin to value that it is disequilibria that keeps us alive, we will find the task quite easy. There is more than enough confusion and ambiguity in our lives to work with. We don't have to worry about creating more, only about how to work more artfully with what we have." From this point of view, we can't control outcomes but we can facilitate the emergence of new patterns.

In my life, one big thunderstorm demanding my attention has been my business career in the infantswear industry.

Our company celebrates its 120th anniversary in 2003 and, though we've been profitable through the years, like most organizations we have experienced highs and lows. E.K.Warren was an inventor, founder of The Warren Featherbone Company, and my great-grandfather. In the first few years of our company's life he had a very difficult time making any money at all. He persisted and was rewarded for that.

Because I knew the end of the story in my first two books, *The Featherbone Principle: A Declaration of Interdependence* and *The Featherbone Spirit: Celebrating Life's Connections,* they were easy to write. They were about the Warren Featherbone Company, established in 1883, and The Warren Featherbone Foundation, established in 1917, and how each survived. This book on renewal has been much more challenging. The very nature of renewal is change that occurs in miraculous and mysterious ways. So, I don't know where this story ends. I believe, though, that for all of us it is in a better place.

As Paul Harvey would say, "and now the rest of the story....". In recent times our business grew, as did the apparel industry. Then, after many years of sales increases, we suffered our first small decline. During the '90s, the apparel industry also experienced a decline. A steadily increasing portion of apparel demand being served by overseas suppliers brought on intense pricing pressure. In 1990, 30% of apparel was imported from countries with wages as low as $1/16$ of US wages; 2002 imported 90%, mainly from the Far East. This trend was not only in apparel. The US Department of Commerce tracks the viability of our industrial base each month through monitoring 22 industrial segments which make up that base. Textiles and apparel is just one of the 22. By 2002, 18 of those 22 industrial segments had developed trade deficits — over 300 BILLION dollars in manufactured products representing the loss of 6 million jobs and hurting communities throughout the country.

Our company's strategy was to replenish products quickly to our retail customers who were predominantly department stores and specialty shops. This strategy proved to be successful, especially when retail partners understood the value of a short supply chain. Their commitment to this concept was rewarded year after year with higher profitability and much greater consumer satisfaction. We could compete in this channel of distribution. Then the channel itself began to collapse. In the late '70s department stores owned 30% of the US apparel market. By 2002, that market share had declined to about 17%. So we were facing both intense pricing pressure and a deteriorating market.

Along with the general economy our sales continued to decline, and for a while it was easy to find reasons for that decline. Our interest was to preserve jobs and in the short term that proved costly. Many employees left the company during this period. That was the most painful. Many nights of little sleep and constant pressure took its toll on all of us. For me, that pressure was manifested in a heart attack. In all of us, heartbreak. What to do? We decided to hang in and find a way to better times. The company had been reinvented at least twice before in its 120-year history. Maybe we could be reinvented again and, in the process, become a renewed people.

In 1999, my brother Bill met Patti Gilmer, a brilliant marketer, entrepreneur, and founder of Future Products Corporation in nearby Alto, Georgia. They saw a connection that would lead directly to that reinvention. Patti and her hardworking business partners pioneered patented flotation swimwear for babies and children known as My Pool Pal™. This innovation was first marketed in 1992. Future Products acquired the rights to the patents and began to grow a new classification of merchandise that was a perfect fit for our company. My Pool Pal™, the flagship brand, was designed specifically for department stores and specialty shops. The Floaty Suit™ was designed for mass merchants, and the Aqua Force™ brand, with 30 % greater buoyancy, was the only US Coast Guard approved swimsuit that could be used in lieu of life jackets for boating. In addition, the American Swim Coaches Association had officially endorsed My Pool Pal™ for use in their **Learn to Swim** program for toddlers. In 2001, Future Products Corporation licensed us the rights to manufacture and market these innovative products. A new company, Alexis PlaySafe, Inc., was created and we were off in a new direction with new energy.

The swimsuits also answered a key concern of our customer base. Grandparents had long been major purchasers of our products. In a written survey conducted by our company almost 10,000 grandparents told us that "safety of my grandchild" was their greatest concern. Our flotation swimwear became part of an emerging umbrella of products that provided water and sun safety for the child and peace of mind for the family. Alexis PlaySafe, Inc., whose mission is "enabling the spirit of play," grew to include *Baby Banz* 100% UV-protected sunglasses from Australia as well as *Baby Blanket Suncare* products. Through these new alliances, each bringing to us innovative products and wonderfully talented people, we were becoming not only a new company but a new highly competitive business model as well.

Good news! Almost immediately we began to grow again. In that growth, however, we also created a substantial need for cash to finance the highly seasonal nature of the new products. At a time when banks were financing few in the apparel industry, Wachovia, the successor to the original Gainesville National Bank and our bank since 1955, saw what we saw and decided to back us. For us it was a frightening and exciting time. As their customer for 50 years, we had loaned them money! Now it was time to borrow money, and lots of it. Wachovia's team worked with us to make it successful. In a particularly poignant moment for me, after expressing our gratitude for all that the bank brought to us, Wachovia's John Cook thoughtfully responded that their interest in us reflected the relationship built by many people in our company over the years. He went on to say that the often-overused term "partnership" was apropos. He and they felt it was time to act like a partner. And they did in the highest and best sense. Our reinvention would not have been possible without them.

Chris Cosper became President and Chief Operating Officer of Alexis PlaySafe, Inc. at its inception. Vic Patterson later became Vice President and CFO. I continued as CEO. The Warren Featherbone Company, now a separate corporation, is the owner of Alexis PlaySafe, Inc. and sponsor of The Warren Featherbone Foundation, which includes a publishing arm. The purpose of the foundation is to raise awareness of the importance of interdependent connections in business and society.

Chris Cosper is the first non-family president of the company in almost 60 years and she has more than met the challenge. Vic Patterson brought strong financial skills and a gift as "change maker." While I have not always been a good leader, I think most of us can spot excellent leadership in others. In working with Chris, Vic, and the team of gifted individuals who joined the company under their leadership, I recognize at least 6 key traits of effective leaders.

1. ***GOOD LEADERS ARE FEARLESS.*** Effective leaders operate from a secure place internally. They are not arrogant, but assured that there are answers and alternative solutions to problems. They prepare meticulously, involve others and work hard. From the start, Vic Patterson impressed me as someone whose attitude was, "I'm not mad, but we are going to address these issues." Predictably, problems *were* solved.

2. ***GOOD LEADERS KNOW HOW TO BUILD A TEAM.*** Determining the team members is a crucial leadership role and should be the number one priority. As a general rule, Chris determined that fewer, more talented players strengthened the team. She looked for the most talented people she could find and made sure they were grounded by good values. She knew that they would attract others just like them to the organization.

3. ***GOOD LEADERS BELIEVE IN THE POWER OF COMMUNICATION.*** Chris started daily 10-15 minute stand-up meetings known as "The Huddle." The idea, suggested by our friend and business advisor, Dan Weston, was for everyone in the meeting (typically 15 departmental

Vic Patterson and Chris Cosper leading the huddle.

leaders) to share with the group two specific pieces of information: their "good news" (personal or business) and their number one priority for the day. Sharing good news immediately and beneficially changes the chemistry in a group. The priorities help the team know quickly each day what each of the other team members is working to complete and, as a result, the efforts of the group are quickly aligned.

4. **GOOD LEADERS KNOW HOW TO ASK THE RIGHT QUESTIONS** and, in doing so, pull together the efforts of all those in the organization. My friend Ken Meyer, business strategist and extraordinary thinker, has developed the Pull Principle™. In his book, *Pull Thinking,* he suggests that we regularly ask the Four Pull Questions about each activity in our organizations: What's the purpose (vision, mission, goal, objective)? What are the measures of success? (What does success look like?) What are the actual measurements? What is the appropriate frequency of the measurements? Clarity on these questions is critical for people to effectively work together.

5. **GOOD LEADERS ARE DECISIVE AND ACTION ORIENTED.** They understand that they can never have all the information before making a decision...but decisions have to be made. Mistakes will be made, of course, but the biggest mistake of all is failure to act.

6. **GOOD LEADERS ARE OPEN TO IDEAS AND FEEDBACK FROM THOSE WITH WHOM THEY WORK.** As a result, the leaders themselves are open to renewal.

Will Alexis PlaySafe, Inc. and The Warren Featherbone Company survive for another 120 years? We don't know exactly the form...we are still inside the chaos/order of evolving shapes. But we believe this chaos is part of a larger orderly pattern. We do know that the original *Featherbone Principle* underscoring the nature of connections keeps all of us in good company. *We are not alone in this world. Whether we recognize it or not, there is an interdependency that exists for us all, corporately, socially and spiritually.* These principles of interdependence and "connectedness" are the very core of who we are.

We all need renewal, a rediscovery of who we are at our core, to successfully deal with our evolving "chaotic-well-ordered" world. We are at our best, and have the most fun in life, when we use the gifts with which we are blessed and when we continue to grow in all areas of our lives.

So what exactly is renewal? How are we renewed? When are we renewed? Who are examples from whom we can learn?

Follow me if you will on a journey of connections, authenticity and renewal. Throughout this book you will meet real people, who in the midst of uncertainty and perceived chaos, embraced life's challenges with an open spirit. They take us on a journey of faith in each other and ourselves. They show us the value of letting go of fear by recognizing our connections with each other discovered in a chance meeting, an illness, a shared experience, a smile or a touch.

This is the gift of renewal.

DIEN DO

Chapter Two

> *"Life is a confrontation between circumstances and character."*
> J.W. FANNING

THESIS OF RENEWAL

IN THE EARLY MORNING OF OCTOBER 1, 2001, the maintenance crew at the Alexis Playsafe plant in Gainesville, Georgia, encountered a problem. As they were attempting to raise the American flag on the front lawn, they discovered the rope was broken. A new rope needed to be threaded through the pulley at the top of the 50-foot flagpole, but none of our ladders reached that far! After a few minutes of head scratching, a number of suggestions were considered including the rental of a "cherry picker" hydraulic lift. It would be expensive and take a while to get onsite, but at the moment it seemed the best option.

Normally making the repair could have waited a while, even a day or two, but because it was less than a month after the tragic events of September 11, patriotism was running high...and getting that flag up there was important. No one knew that more than Dien Do, a valued employee in the shipping department at Alexis PlaySafe. As a captain in the South Vietnamese army during the Vietnam conflict, he had fought alongside our American soldiers and was imprisoned by the North Vietnamese for seven years. In the mid-'90s, he and his wife emigrated to the United States to experience a freedom he never knew in his native country. Like others around him that morning, he understood perfectly well what the American flag stands for and why getting that rope threaded was something that needed to be done.

Dien also knew how to get it done. Quietly he removed his shoes and socks and, with the rope in his mouth, shinnied up the flagpole. He tried threading the rope but it wouldn't fit. No problem for Dien — he just climbed down, let the maintenance crew tape the end and back up he went. This time it worked, and within a few minutes the flag was flying high again over the Alexis PlaySafe property. Dien, at the age of 60, stood proudly beneath.

In the grand scheme of world events this was not a headline story, but *The Times*, our Gainesville newspaper, did write it up. For the small, awestruck group gathered there that morning, it was a moment they could not wait to tell the rest of us about. We all came to believe that something very special had happened that morning. Something beyond admiration for Dien or even

DIEN DO

pride in our flag. It was something deeper, something much better. We were renewed.

If you look up the word "renew" in the dictionary, you find a couple of definitions that you would expect: "to make like new" or "restore to freshness." But there are a couple of other meanings that are particularly interesting: "to make new spiritually," " regenerate," and "to restore to existence; revive." The notions of physical and non-physical regeneration contained in those definitions are especially relevant to

> **re-new** (rĭ-nōō', -nyōō) *v. -newed, -newing, -news.* — *tr* **1.** To make new as if new again; restore to freshness. **2.** To make new spiritually. **3.** Regenerate. **4.** To restore to existence; revive. **5.** To replenish. **6.** To bring into being again. **7.** To take up again; resume. **8.** To repeat so as to reaffirm.

this book's thesis of renewal, and they help explain why we think the subject is worthy of exploration.

We know intuitively that we need renewal. Physically, we are constantly being renewed without even trying. The cell structures in our bodies are programmed for it. As old body cells die they are continuously replaced by new ones at the rate of millions of cells per second. It is amazing to think that our bodies are renewing themselves on their own, and so rapidly. Did you know, for example, that the linings in our mouths are completely renewed every three days? Our intestinal linings are renewed every five days; our respiratory linings every eleven days. Within six months we have a whole new bloodstream. And, believe it or not, within two years we have a new bone structure. Basically, we have all new bodies every seven years.

As important as it is, renewal doesn't end with the physical. We need non-physical renewal as well, especially in this age of stress and burnout. In an interview with Larry King recently, Dr. James Dobson, founder of Focus on the Family, stated that the breakup of the family is more about burnout than anything else. By the end of the day, he says, we're simply too exhausted to relate to our spouses and our children. Whether it's a result of pressures at work or pressures at home, burnout can be a dangerous, downward spiral. It often continues day in and day out until one day we wake up and realize we're missing out on the best that life has to offer.

Although burnout does not seem to be a neat diagnostic category in psychiatry books, it is still a topic of much research and discussion among psychologists and psychiatrists. Dr. Michael H. Gendel, M.D., associate professor of psychiatry at the University of Colorado Health Sciences Center, has produced over a hundred articles on the subject and cites the major symptom of burnout as detachment from relationships, along with exhaustion and loss of satisfaction or sense of accomplishment. When we reach the point of burnout we withdraw from others, we stagnate, and we escape into the privacy of our couches in front of the television. If good relationships demand that we stay connected to each other, you can see how burnout can be a real problem in family relationships.

If burnout causes us to deteriorate spiritually, which can eventually cause trouble for us physically, then what we need is renewal. Like a stagnant creek that needs fresh water flowing through it, we need replenishment in our souls. To live our lives fully, we need to experience regeneration. We need to be made new, restored to freshness, invigorated. But how? Our thesis for this book is that non-physical renewal is brought to us by other people. Dien Do serves as a great example. He was an agent of renewal. Through his simple (not that I could do it) act of climbing that flagpole and repairing that rope, he brought renewal to us. Those who were there and all of us who heard about it that morning experienced it. It was a teaching moment, and in the moment we were inspired. But more than that, we were transformed. Re-energized. Renewed.

Through our work and personal relationships, we all have the opportunity to experience renewal through people we meet. This book is all about those renewing agents who appear in our midst. Like Dien Do, who surprised us with his talent and boldness, they often come unexpectedly...sometimes out of obscurity...to center stage. Before Dien Do climbed the pole, we really did not know him well. Now we'll never forget him.

In the following chapters of this book, you will enjoy reading the remarkable stories of some extraordinary people and organizations I have had the privilege of knowing. I think you'll be inspired by their courage, their wisdom, their dreams, and their passion. Each story represents another principle and another step along the journey toward renewal. Some of the stories and ideas will make you laugh, some will inspire you, and all may cause you to think...and even re-think, which is itself an open door to renewal. Mostly, I hope that through these stories you will make a connection and experience some degree of renewal in your own life.

KATHRYN SMITH

Chapter Three

*"In order to make a break for freedom,
you have to unload many burdens."*
DAVID WHYTE, WELSH POET

LETTING GO

KATHRYN SMITH AND I HAVE WORKED TOGETHER FOR YEARS. She has been my co-worker, counselor, and friend. I had just become chairman/chief executive of Alexis PlaySafe, Incorporated. My previous position as president was being filled by Chris Cosper, who was moving down the hall. Then it hit me! The president belongs in the president's office, and it was time for me to move and establish a new office. So, after 24 years in the same office, Kathryn and I began the process of moving out.

Let me tell you about Kathryn. She has wisdom and intensity. It's best not to get caught between her and something that needs to get done. We look back and remember the time we spent moving my office as "dumpster days." We started by reading and gingerly removing 24 year-old files, which I'm sure contained tens of thousands of pieces. And it wasn't moving fast enough for us. I had to let go. So I did. Pretty soon whole files were in the air on the way to the dumpster. It felt good to be traveling lighter by the minute.

Then we came to old photos and plaques on the walls. It was difficult to part with any of that. So much of me was invested in them. Kathryn was wonderfully relentless. Said she, "These have to go." "But, Kathryn," I replied, "if we throw these out how will I know how great I am?" To which she responded with a twinkle in her eye, "I'm going to tell you every day." Wham! Two more for the dumpster. And they were gone. It's hard, but necessary, to let go if you are truly to be renewed.

Why is it hard to let go? I guess it's because we get so comfortable with the old. As president, I loved solving problems and putting out fires. I did that for all those years and, in my new role, I missed the thrill of fighting fires. Fear of the future...the unknown...is also a powerful emotion that causes us to hold on tenaciously to the past.

My friends, Mary Lynn and John Coyle, say that everyone should quit most of their activities every five years and then add back only the ones that are appropriate for the "emerging you." Great advice. And who is the emerging you?

What are you becoming and what is your unique gift? Business writer Jim Collins, in his best seller *Good to Great*, tells us how to know what we should be doing in life. Find the intersection of three circles:

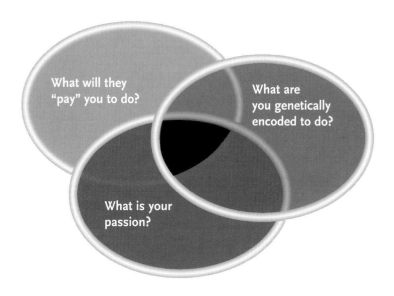

It's the intersection of those circles that tell us where we should be and what we probably need to eliminate.

Letting go and life simplification are necessary for renewal. My pastor, Dr. Bill Coates, says that life simplification is about "getting rid of...not better organizing...too much." I like that thought. Over the years my wife, Nell, and I have tried to simplify. For about six years when our children were very young we literally removed the television from our home during the spring and summer months. That simplification ensured much better family time. TV watching is a surprisingly easy habit to give up. Almost anything you replace it with is likely to be a better investment of your family's time. And at the same time you eliminate the background noise of the TV set, which is just another form of pollution. It's like the exit of an unwelcome visitor. Try it.

Here are some other ways I have found to simplify my life:

1. **PAY BILLS ONCE A MONTH.** If you're married, pay them with your spouse.
2. **IF YOU CAN'T PAY CASH FOR IT, DON'T BUY IT.** Homes excluded.
3. **BE SELECTIVE IN YOUR TIME COMMITMENTS.** An open calendar is a good thing. Learn to say no.
4. **DONATE HALF OF YOUR CLOTHING TO CHARITY.**
5. **CLEAR OUT CLUTTER – CLOSETS, DESKS, AND SO ON.**
6. **PRIORITIZE YOUR DAY** and start by sending a thank-you

note to someone.

7. **UPDATE OR WRITE YOUR WILL** and deal with unsettled interpersonal issues.

8. **GET A PHYSICAL.**

9. **TAKE A SABBATICAL**… at least find a quiet time every day.

10. **DONATE THE OTHER HALF OF YOUR CLOTHING.**

Why all this attention to simplification? As we are renewed, there is only so much we can take with us. Welsh poet and author, David Whyte, believes that "in order to make a break for freedom, you have to unload many burdens." We must constantly grow, and that growth often takes place from the new open areas in our lives. It's almost like the fires in the forest. They are necessary to let in the light so that the seeds that have been in that forest all along can germinate. Creative destruction is a seemingly contradictory term that is a part of renewal. It breathes new life into us. Naturalist John Muir writes:

"Climb the mountains and get their good tidings.
Nature's peace will flow into you
as sunshine flows into trees.
The winds will blow their own freshness into you,
And the storms their energy
While cares drop off like autumn leaves."

This brings me to the need for dealing with worry. Worry has plagued me most of my life. At the base of that is fear, of course. Fear of failure, rejection, being embarrassed, and so forth. Lots of reasons to fear and that's no way to live. J.W. Fanning, former Vice President of the University of Georgia, co-founder of Leadership Georgia, and a wonderful mentor in my life had this to say about fear:

"A life built around fear is terrible.
To fear is to live backwards. To have faith is to live forward.
A life built around faith is a magnificent thing."

I like the idea that fear is really only "**f**alse **e**vidence **a**ppearing **r**eal." I have always found it easy to find that evidence. One thing I've learned since my heart attack is that you can look death straight in the face and not be afraid. I'm sure faith has a lot to do with that. Many people have had that experience. If we can face death and not worry, what about those daily urgent crises that are rarely important in the long run? I like the following Irish conundrum.

"There is no need to worry....
If you are doing all you can about something,
there is no need to worry because
you are doing all you can about it.
If there is nothing you can do about something,
there is no need to worry because
there is nothing you can do about it. Therefore...
There is no need to worry."

Well, that explanation does not always bring comfort. What does for me, though, is the thought that we are all made by God as uniquely gifted people. When we renew those unique gifts in each other and when those gifts are used for the greater good, there is in fact no reason to worry. Why? Because we aren't the giver of those gifts. The gifts are given through us by a creative life force, however we might define that force. And in that context worry simply cannot exist. Worry has never been a part of creation. Thus, its absence is also at the heart of renewal.

Lee Lathrop

Chapter Four

*"Be not forgetful to entertain strangers: for thereby
some have entertained angels unawares."*
HEBREWS 13:2

RENEWAL IN ACTION

What does renewal look like? Often we do not recognize a gift of renewal until one day we realize that our lives have been transformed by it. This is the awesome power of renewal in action.

In 1994 I met Lee Lathrop, who at that time served as Director of Executive Communications at The Boeing Company in Seattle. I worked together with Lee and Phil Condit (Boeing's CEO) to plan for Boeing's acceptance of the Manufacturer of the Year Award presented by The Warren Featherbone Foundation. Lee also helped Phil and me develop the foreword for my first book, *The Featherbone Principle*. I was first impressed with Lee's organizational gifts, but even more by his sincerity and thoughtfulness. He is a deep thinker and an accomplished writer in his own right.

Over the years I've stayed in touch with Lee. We have one of those unique connections, the kind where we are on the same page when we reconnect. Through the years I've always felt encouraged by him and felt a sense of being renewed. So when I received word that his wife had passed away I sent a card and made a point to visit him on my next trip to Seattle.

When I shared with Lee our plans for this book, he felt we were on the right track and offered his help. More than that, he offered his own story of how he had been renewed by someone who unexpectedly entered his life at just the right time. The following account of Lee's newfound friend, Ole, is a heartfelt example of how others can bring renewal to us…and we to them.

Ole's Story

By Lee Lathrop

Young Olan Oberg came into my life like a flash of light that swept away a darkness that had closed around me due to personal illness and the sudden loss of my wife of 42 years.

My cancer had gone into remission and my strength was just returning when Peggy died of heart failure. I owe a lot to doctors, nurses and new treatments for my recovery, but Peggy was the real reason I survived. She dedicated more than a year to my recovery but, when her time came, I was helpless.

Family, friends and neighbors rallied around to help. But they were grieving too, and I did my best to put on a happy face. Our two children were of special comfort, yet they too needed my support in order to deal with the loss of their mother.

When everyone went home, when the food was eaten and the roomful of flowers started to fade, the silence was heavy. Everything in the house brought memories of Peggy to the surface. It was springtime, and her flower gardens came to life. But what should have been the happiest of memories brought only despair and tears.

We had left Seattle five years before, just before my

retirement, and moved 100 miles south, buying a home and a few acres of land in the country near the small town of Toledo, Washington. After a long career of working in offices I enjoyed the physical labor of keeping up the land, planting gardens and mowing a little more than two acres of the property.

With Peggy's death came the additional chore of keeping up the house. I needed help. Janice, one of my neighbors, came by now and then to help weed the gardens. It was Janice who brought Olan to my house one day while he was visiting her son. Olan, or Ole as his family and friends call him, came to ask me for a job to earn some pocket money.

Ole lives on a family farm near the Cowlitz River with his parents and three younger siblings...a sister and two brothers. He works hard on the farm, performing a long list of chores morning and evening. Ole's parents Eric and Rebecca have taught him useful skills and he has a work ethic rarely found in adults, let alone in a 12-year-old boy.

He feeds a large herd of goats hay and grain twice a day and feeds the baby goats their milk. He sometimes helps with the milking, and pasteurizes the milk. Ole also feeds all the cattle several bales of hay a day during the winter, and feeds the calves their milk. He personally owns and raises two steers each year. Ole has 30 chickens, and twice a day he collects and washes the eggs. Some of them even lay blue or green eggs. He feeds and cares for two mares on the farm.

OLAN OBERG

Ole feeds his goats

During the summer he and his sister and brothers grow strawberries, which they sell to neighbors.

This year the three oldest Oberg children, Ole, Linnea, 11, and Torre, 6, showed animals in the Lewis County 4-H Youth Fair. All three won top prizes. Ole showed one of the goats that he is training as a pack animal. The youngest child, Lars, 3, isn't quite ready to participate.

On the day Ole came to ask for work, I asked him what he could do for me. He said, "I could drive our F350 truck when I was five. I drove it while my dad threw gravel from the back to fix the road. I learned to drive a four-wheeler at my grandparents' farm, and started hauling logs and wood and ran errands. Mowing grass is fun. But what I really like to do is work on motors and farm machinery. I'm going to be a mechanic." He wasn't bragging, just giving me the facts.

His steel-blue eyes looked right at me as he made his case. When it was my turn to talk, he still held eye contact and listened carefully. The only sign of nervousness was a slight squeaking of his sneakers on the floor. We came to terms on the spot.

And so Ole started coming around every week or so to mow grass. In between mowing, he worked on my motorized gardening equipment, getting them running after they had sat idle during my illness. He didn't say much, but just kept working and thinking of new and better ways to do his jobs.

When I decided to build a greenhouse, Ole's first contribution to that effort was to move a pile of bricks to the site so we could lay a floor. I advised him to use a wheelbarrow, but after one trip with that I think he decided that it was silly to load the wheelbarrow, move it, then unload it. So he ran back and forth with armloads of bricks. What he lacked in capacity he made up for in speed.

It was a two-person, two-day job assembling the greenhouse. The first day I drove the screws while Ole acted as the "gofer." On the second day, he beat me to the drill that we used to drive the screws, so I became the "gofer" and he did the assembly. He wanted to have a bigger role in the finished product. He was more methodical than I and the result was better.

Ole always finds the positive side of situations. Once when he discovered that I had bought the wrong replacement spool for my weeder, he comforted me by saying, "Oh, well. The spool is a good place to store the cord."

What was apparent from the first was Ole's spiritual side. He's very devout, and when he eats lunch at my house he always gives thanks to God for the food and even for the opportunity to work on my machinery and land. I knew that his parents also were devout folks, but there was something else about Ole that I couldn't quite understand. He combined his spirituality with a zest for life. He loved animals and sometimes he would spend most of a day watching birds around the farm. He seemed to appreciate everything about this world while most youngsters are prone to take it for granted. Where did this come from in one so young?

On the Fourth of July the Obergs invited me to a cookout and picnic on the farm with their extended family. There I learned that Ole had entered this life in difficulty. He was born with a serious heart defect. When only seventeen months old, he had open-heart surgery. This was followed by other operations, the last when he was six. His family said that after that crucial surgery, an entirely new Ole emerged. His great spirit developed then as he fought to live a normal life. Now, on the cusp of becoming a teenager, he is an energetic healthy young man who is thankful for every day of life. I knew that Ole had accepted me as a friend when I was invited to come to his church one Sunday evening to hear him and his Vacation Bible School group sing songs for family and friends. He was easy to spot among the bobbing young heads on the stage as the energetic youngsters belted out rousing, hand-clapping spiritual songs. He was the only one wearing a bright John Deere cap. Our friendship was further sealed when my son took Ole and me fishing on his new boat at a local lake. The usually calm and quiet Ole became very animated and talkative after landing two nice Coho salmon.

Ole is determined to attend a special John Deere Company school that is designed to train young people in farm machinery repair. There's a shortage of good farm mechanics as young people answer the siren call of the high-tech, high-wages world. John Deere won't find a better candidate than Ole.

A few days before I sat down to write this, I was fixing lunch while Ole zipped around my yard on the lawn tractor. The mower motor stopped and Ole soon appeared in the kitchen holding up a broken drive belt. His barely contained smile melted away my scowl as he contemplated his favorite activity — repairing a tractor. To nurture his love of machinery, Ole and his mother are restoring two old tractors as a hobby.

Besides becoming a mechanic, Ole's dreams include owning a small farm, just like several previous generations of the Oberg family. Wise beyond his years, he thinks that he might have two to four children. "But," he adds, "that's something I'll have to talk over with my wife."

Ole has taught me many lessons about appreciating life and being thankful for it. It is all the proof I need that spiritual renewal comes to us from others, even from someone 54 years younger. Not by anything he has said, but just by the way he lives his life, Ole has become my spiritual role model and the medicine that I needed to heal my grief.

Now when I see something that reminds me of Peggy, I feel good about the memory, and can even laugh at some of the funny things that happened to us.

I don't think it was just by chance that Ole came to my house when he did.

Peggy, if you can hear me up there...did you have any-thing to do with this?

DAVID SLOYER

Chapter Five

*"The greatest learning and creativity
take place on the edge of chaos."*
DEB WHITEHOUSE, AUTHOR / SPEAKER

IT'S THE JOURNEY,
NOT THE DESTINATION

In 1965 a slender 25-year-old man named David Sloyer exited a bus in downtown Atlanta and wandered into the El Mexicano Restaurant. He was fresh into town from California and drawn to the place. The El Mexicano, located a block south of the Fox Theater, was operated by the Aguilar family, whose friendly spirit and good food made him feel welcome. David bonded with them immediately and knew he would come back.

When he first tasted it that day, David knew that Guido Aguilar's homemade salsa concoction was something special. Had he known then what the next thirty years held for him, he might have given serious thought to packaging the stuff and selling it. But David was not about marketing a food product. He worked for Lockheed, (today, Lockheed Martin Corporation)...and his real ambition was racing sports cars.

"When I came to work for Lockheed in 1965, I didn't know anybody from Atlanta, and I didn't even know where Marietta was," David recalls. "I was only 25, but I already had a heck of a resume. I was making good money and driving a Porsche. I made friends with a guy named Earl Walker and we started racing sports cars at weekend races in Ohio, Savannah, and elsewhere. We would leave work on Friday, drive all night to an event, practice on Saturday, race on Sunday, then drive all the way back Sunday night in time to be at work on Monday morning."

Racing was in their blood, but the two young friends eventually had to admit that the schedule was just too grueling. Driving back one night from a weekend trip to Ohio, exhausted from the experience, they talked about finding a better way to live their dream. From that conversation a crazy idea was born. They would build their own racetrack somewhere near Atlanta.

"Nobody believed we would do it or that a sports car race track could succeed in Georgia. We worked out details on the back of napkins at the El Mexicano," David laughs. "I had become good friends with Guido and his family. Over the years that's where a lot of my ideas originated. That's where the name Road Atlanta was born. "

Road Atlanta was built in 1970 with investments from such Atlanta notables as Arthur Montgomery, who at the time owned the Atlanta Coca-Cola Bottling Company and was a primary investor in the old Atlanta Fulton County Stadium. David and Earl were committed to making Road Atlanta a profitable venture but in those early years they ran into a number of unexpected hurdles, not the least of which was a crippling gasoline crisis.

"Then an accident killed a spectator at a local drag strip, so suddenly sponsors wouldn't touch racing," David explains. "We kept at it but it was tough. Eventually, Arthur and other investors assumed controlling interest and hired Earl and me to do the work. Then Earl left and I ran it until the late '70s when it was sold to the new owners."

The new owners, as it turned out, had other plans for the race venue and as a result David made his decision to leave racing altogether. It was not a happy decision. Giving up his brainchild and his passion for racing, especially under such dark circumstances, hurt him deeply. The months following were painful. He had no future, no further aspirations. He had come to the first big roadblock in his life's journey. Literally.

"So I went to Costa Rica," David recalls. "I stayed with a friend of Guido's, a man who was the second largest coffee producer in the country. He was a millionaire with a large home. It was a beautiful place, but I was single at the time and lonely. One day after I had been there a while, sitting by the pool, I realized that I was 3000 miles from home and nobody even knew I was there. And more than that, nobody really cared."

It was a moment of self-realization for David. He returned to the States with a desire to find his destiny. But at first he could only find work at a wrecking yard making deliveries and operating a wrecker. Less than a year later he left that job to work the parts and service counter at a BMW repair shop in Atlanta. In his heart, David knew that both jobs were a means to an end...but he still had no idea what that end was.

Coming back home brought more significant changes to David's life than just work. He met Linda, married, and gained a lifelong partner. He also met a man who introduced him to the world of marketing, Amway style.

"He was a customer at the BMW shop and he invited me and my wife, Linda, to his home to learn about selling Amway products. Linda got into the business first. She sponsored me and we got started. It was absolutely the best thing that had happened to me because of what I learned. I listened to hundreds of motivational tapes and read books like *Think and Grow Rich*. I couldn't get enough, and I still have two or three hundred audio tapes."

Through the mid to late '80s, David and Linda experienced success with Amway, although David didn't advance that far in the system. However, he did learn a lot about meeting people and sales. Those skills were a major advantage in his next ventures, marketing water filters for National Safety Associates and later, in the early '90s, helping build a company called Amtech. Then, on August 24, 1994, David Sloyer's life took a dramatic and unexpected turn.

"We were sleeping on our boat at Lake Lanier," David recalls. "In the middle of the night I woke up thinking I had to go to the bathroom. When I stood up I nearly fainted. I managed to make it to the bathroom and, when I got inside, I threw up… and when I did, blood went everywhere. I went to my knees, then reached back and slammed the door to wake Linda."

Linda woke up to the bloody sight and thought for a moment that David had been blasted with a shotgun. She managed to get him back to the bed, then went for help. Thankfully the boat was docked so she didn't have to go far. A night man at the guard house called an ambulance that miraculously was making its way down Georgia 400, just a few miles from the lake. Within an hour or so, David was transported to Northside Hospital in Atlanta.

Two weeks of numerous biopsies and tests revealed that David had liver disease. The bloody eruption on his boat had been the result of capillaries in his esophagus bursting, a side effect of the disease, which the doctors officially diagnosed as cryptogenic liver disease. The initial remedy called for David to change his diet and hope that it would heal itself. But by January of 1995, after his weight dropped from 170 to 140 pounds and his deteriorating health became increasingly apparent, the doctors at Emory University Hospital determined that he had end stage liver disease.

"I asked them what that meant, and they told me I would have to have a transplant or I would die," remembers David. "I told them 'I'm not gonna die, so tell me what's next.'"

What came next was the frustrating wait for a liver donor. The waiting list was long and the possible donors few. His health continued to deteriorate but all he could do was hope for his turn to come.

"I was terribly sick. Sometimes it was so painful, sitting in the bathroom bleeding internally, I just wanted to die right there. It's tough even now to relive it. I remember reading in the Bible where Jesus says 'I will never leave you nor forsake you', and thinking that I could either go with him or something is going to have to happen. But I kept losing weight and getting weaker. I was at home all day not doing anything except thinking about dying so I began to pray to God to give me something to do. Then one night I woke up thinking about Guido's salsa. I don't know why. Guido had already closed El Mexicano, but I called him the next day and asked him if he wanted to bottle his salsa. He told me that after he closed the restaurant he'd had a hundred phone calls asking him to make his salsa for special occasions. So he was still making this great salsa but he said he didn't know how to market it. I told him I didn't either, but I could sure figure it out. And that's how we got started."

Marketing Guido's salsa became David's full-time occupation, even though he had virtually no experience in the food industry. All he knew for sure was that Guido's salsa was an exceptional product and, if he could get it marketed and distributed somehow, it had a good chance for success. Even in his weakened physical state David managed to get the ball rolling. From Jim Hindy, a generous friend who knew of his condition, he got a quality computer on which he could hammer out label designs, conduct the necessary research, and develop a nutrition statement and other paperwork requirements for marketing a food product. Suddenly, in spite of his rapidly deteriorating health, David Sloyer was on a mission.

But time was running out. Every Wednesday David would visit the specialists at Emory University Hospital and gather more reports about his condition. He made copies of all of his records and learned as much as he could about the disease. The blood counts told the story. He was on the very edge of death. On one visit his doctor looked at his incredibly low blood count and his frail body and asked him how he was able to even stand. Concerned that he could go at any moment, the doctor took action.

On September 30, 1995, David was sitting in a lawn chair in his back yard, barely able to move. Afraid that he might not make it through the day, Linda had stayed home. It was a beautiful day so she had helped him outside to the chair. Then the phone in his lap rang.

"It was the pre-transplant coordinator telling me they had found a liver. I don't know where the energy came from, but I came up out of that chair and told Linda they wanted me down there in two hours. I called Bill Grant, a great friend who worked for the Georgia State Patrol, and within minutes we jumped into his car and off we went to the hospital. During my Road Atlanta days, I had contracted with the Georgia State Patrol to train troopers in high-speed pursuit. So all the way down to the hospital we're laughing and talking…not about my transplant, but about racing."

The liver transplant was supposed to last about five or six hours. David was on the operating table for 12. At one early point during the operation the doctors reported to Linda that lesions around the liver were making it extremely dangerous to remove the liver. They couldn't guarantee success. After some discussion with family members, it was agreed that David would be disappointed if they did not try. Linda gave the doctor the go-ahead. Within 45 minutes they had the liver removed. A few hours later, the transplant was complete.

Within three days of the operation David began walking. Within 12 days he was back home. In November, just a little over a month after his transplant operation, he joined a fitness center. His registered weight was 110 pounds. He could barely move 80 pounds on the weight machine. But David Sloyer had faced imminent death and apparently won back his life.

"Thanks to the incredible performance of the doctors and nurses at Emory, especially my surgeon, Dr. André Stieber, my recovery was fast. Over the next two years, I gained weight and improved dramatically. I continued to build the salsa business, selling mostly to 'mom and pop' stores, individuals and mail order. The first big sale came in 1998, to Harris Teeter grocery stores. They put us in nine stores with the product which was called Guido's Gourmet Salsa."

David pressed Harris Teeter's buyers to offer Guido's Salsa in all 145 stores but they were concerned with the brand name. Among other things, consumers often made the mistake of thinking the name Guido was Italian.

"So we considered what kind of investment we would have to make in changing the name," David says. "Ultimately we decided to change it to Sarchi, which comes from the name of a town in Costa Rica. It's an Aztec word that actually means 'under the volcano.' Sarchi sits at the base of a volcano and is a neat little arts and crafts village. We changed the whole look and design of the salsa brand in thirty days. We thought we might lose some business in the process, but we didn't."

By 2002, at the writing of this book, Sarchi Salsa is being distributed to 350 stores in the Southeast including Harris Teeter, Ingle's, Kroger, Lowe's Foods, Harry's Farmers Market, and a host of smaller grocery stores. With that kind of volume the company was in a position to build its own factory in North Georgia, which in turn allows Sarchi to maintain competitive pricing and grow. In just a few years, Sarchi Salsa under David's leadership has carved out a significant niche in the gourmet salsa market. And the future could not look brighter. A growing market for the Sarchi product has emerged, and no wonder. It really is an extraordinary salsa!

After all of his life's adventures, David Sloyer's journey still has legs. He did more than just survive. He overcame. Sometimes it seems that certain people face more than their share of difficult circumstances. David Sloyer certainly had his fair share. But it hasn't been without a great reward.

"I am a better person for having gone through all that I went through," David says emphatically. "I understand more. I'm a kinder person. Back in the Road Atlanta days, you might not have liked my attitude, which was 'lead, follow or get out of the way.' But I wouldn't do that today."

"I am a better person for having gone through the transplant experience. I think it was the continuation of saying to myself, 'I'm not going to give up until it's time to go.'

My faith said to me, 'God has something for you to do.' I don't know what that is, exactly, but I don't think it's just about the salsa. It may be nothing more than to just go around telling people my story."

And that's precisely what David Sloyer enjoys doing most, it seems. During a store demo recently, David was approached by a man who asked him how he got started in the business. "So I told him my story. We talked and talked, and I bet he stayed there an hour. His daughter was ready to go, but he just did not want to stop talking. Then he told me how much he appreciated my taking the time to talk to him. His wife had died the week before and he felt alone with his two young daughters. 'I'm not sick and I'm not dying,' he told me. 'I've lost my wife, but there's no reason I can't keep going on.' Then he shook my hand and walked away."

Later, David related the incident to Linda, who wisely suggested, "Maybe that's what God wants you to do."

David Sloyer was renewed physically in a dramatic and remarkable way. Without that new liver, he was a goner. With it, he had renewed strength and energy to carry on an extended life. And, as exciting as it is, that physical renewal is only half of David Sloyer's story. The other part of the story is his remarkable non-physical renewal. The renewal that turned him into a "better person." The renewal that allows him to honestly say it isn't about making a million selling salsa, or even about being broke. It seems that David has come to understand on a somewhat deeper level what his life is all about.

"It might sound trite, but it truly is about the journey," David summarizes. "I've learned there's nothing you can do about yesterday. No matter what along the journey you did, good or bad, it is gone. And there's nothing you can do about tomorrow. It is about now. That is all we can control."

So much credit for David's non-physical renewal goes to those people who loved and supported him through the difficult moments in his journey – his wife, Linda, his business partner, Michael Dowda, the Aguilar family, the friend who lent him the computer, the state trooper who rushed him to the hospital, and others. People are agents of renewal when their lives touch ours in a positive way. David Sloyer's life story touches us in a positive way because, like the man in the grocery store, we see our own lives from a new perspective. That sad and lonely father walked out of the store that day renewed by David's story.

Perhaps you will be renewed by it, too.

"Don't search for the answers,

which could not be given to you now,

because you would not be able to live them.

And the point is, to live everything.

Live the questions now.

Perhaps then, someday far in the future,

you will gradually,

without even knowing it,

live your way into the answer."

RANIER MARIA RILKE
LETTERS TO A YOUNG POET
LETTER 4

Robin Davie

Chapter Six

*"We shall not cease from exploration
and the end of all our exploring
will be to arrive where we started
and know the place for the first time."*
T. S. ELIOT

SURVIVING THE CALMS

omewhere out on the vast Atlantic Ocean near the equator, alone on a 50-foot sailboat, 48-year-old Robin Davie faced one of the greatest struggles of his many years at sea. It was late in the year 1998, and the salty, seagoing veteran from Cornwall, England, was on the first leg of the 1998 Around Alone sailboat race, perhaps the most dangerous and challenging of all international competitions. On any given day or night of the 27,000-mile voyage, gale force winds can hurtle a skipper's boat about for hours or days on end. A mast or rudder can break, sails can be torn asunder, or the boat can capsize or run aground on a sandbar. When least expected, a friendly ocean can become an unrelenting and merciless adversary.

But none of those potential calamities worried Robin Davie so much. He had a bigger problem. He was in the calms.

"They drive you absolutely nuts," says Robin. "During the calms, you can't sleep, not even for an hour, or you'll miss that little gust of wind that might carry you forward 100 yards or so. You have to stay alert, day after day, hour after hour, minute by minute. If I do sleep, I set my alarm – a very loud firebell – to wake me every 15 minutes. It drives you absolutely nuts."

The calms, otherwise known as "doldrums," is a windless band near the equator that all sailors dread. It is the complete absence of wind and storms. When you are in the calms, you are powerless. The race is still on, but you don't feel like you are racing at all. You have lost momentum and you are helpless to do anything to change the situation.

We all experience "the calms" in our lives. Think of those periods when the world is racing past us while we seem to be standing still. Maybe the calms come in the form of slow times in our businesses, or stagnated relationships, or periods of spiritual dryness. In any of those cases, we need fresh wind in our sails. Until we get it, we sit and wait helplessly. And as Robin says, it can drive you absolutely nuts.

I first met Robin through a connection related to my work with the South Carolina Research Authority, SCRA. Dr. John Bradham, a great friend who is a leader in that research organization and someone who enjoys making connections as much as I do, suggested I meet Robin and hear his remarkable story. We met for breakfast one morning in Charleston, and Robin told us about himself. What a story! It was packed with drama and risk-taking adventure. Like other stories in this book, it serves to inspire us in our own life adventures. And the lessons and principles we can gain from it might help us better understand the steps in our journey toward renewal. We asked Robin to share with us the primary lessons he has learned from his experiences. Below he shares his top six on the list:

1. **MAKE IT TO THE STARTING LINE.** The 1998 race was not Robin's first. He had raced in both the 1991 and 1994 competitions and, though he did not win, he finished both times, in and of itself a major accomplishment. Today, Robin is one of a select group who can say they have sailed around the world alone three times. But Robin is quick to point out that his quest to win the Around Alone began long before his first race in 1991. In fact, he had labored most of his adult life just trying to get to the starting line.

After more than twenty years of planning, training, boat building and money raising, he finally found himself in the race in 1991. For this 1991 competition there were about 500 inquiries to the race office. Those were all the people who genuinely thought they could be in the race. There were 56 actual entries, and only 28 made it to the starting line. Robin didn't win in 1991, but only 18 sailors finished and Robin was one of them.

2.   ***EXPECT THE UNEXPECTED.*** During the second leg of the 1998 race Robin experienced a broken rudder, a diesel fuel leak, and a long list of other problems. He says, "One piece of advice I give to anyone sailing in this race is to expect the unexpected. Hope for the best but plan for the worst, so that no matter what happens you'll still get to the next port and, most importantly, stay in the race."

3.   ***TAKE EACH DAY AS IT COMES.*** "You have to treat each day as being as good as it gets," he advises. "It doesn't matter how bad it is on any particular day, that's what you've got that day. If you look at the entire 27,000 miles of the race, you wouldn't want to bloody well do it. So you break it down: Charleston to Bermuda, Bermuda to the equator, and so on. When it gets really bad, you break it down into that day, and sometimes it comes down to asking yourself if you can deal with the next hour. There were some days when it was so bad that I literally banged my head against the table. And yet a half-hour later I would go outside to cool off with a cup of tea, and there would be a rainbow, or a whale blowing off in the distance, or a fantastic waterspout coming out of the clouds. There's always something

spectacular on the sea, twenty-four hours a day."

4. ***BRING EVERYTHING DOWN TO A MANAGEABLE LEVEL.*** "When you set sail out of Dover, England, and look at your radar screen, you might see 140 ships. There are so many you can't see your way through them, especially when it's pitch black and they're all going in different directions. What you have to do is adjust your radar screen down to just a half-mile range. Now you see only 10 ships instead of 140, and you work your way around those. Then you see the next 10 and you work your way around those. It's a matter of bringing things down to a manageable level."

5. ***REDEFINE WINNING.*** In the 1998 race, Robin was disqualified after the leg that ended in Auckland, New Zealand. He had experienced serious damage to his boat, he was physically and mentally spent, and there was just not enough money available for the extensive repairs needed. "We decided to continue the race, to persevere, even though we knew we were going to lose, officially." After 35 days in Auckland he was more than 40 days behind the rest of the fleet when he finally sailed off on the third leg to Punta del Este in Uruguay. Remarkably, that leg was as disaster free as the previous one had been disastrous. As it turned out, another competitor was dismasted early in the fourth leg and had

returned to Punta del Este to get a new one. He left for Charleston about the same time that Robin did. It suddenly became a competitive opportunity the two skippers couldn't resist, and the fourth leg became a race between the two of them.

In May of 1999, Robin Davie sailed his boat into Charleston Harbor. Incredibly, although he had been disqualified, he had caught up with the fleet and followed them across the finish line. By his own definition, he was still a winner.

6. ***LEARN HOW TO SURVIVE THE CALMS.*** When he reflects on all the dangers of racing in the Around Alone, in spite of what you might expect, Robin believes the most dangerous part of the race happens when you reach the calms.

"If you can get through the calms, you can make it," he says. "It's really a mind game. You think to yourself, 'I'm not getting anywhere. My competition is overtaking me.' After a few days in the calms the temptation is to give up completely. But you can't do that. There are always zephyrs of wind, even if you can't feel them. You must have the discipline to keep sailing *just as if there were wind*. And you must remember that the wind probably won't come to get you. You have to sail yourself out of the calms."

And so it is in life. Lack of adversity can often be our greatest adversary. In our search for change and renewal, our efforts often seem to be producing nothing. We are tempted to give up. Or we expect things to get better on their own. What we need to realize is that the wind is always blowing, at least a little. We must have that faith. We must put up our sails and believe that our efforts will be propelled by the tiny zephyrs of wind into the future we are sailing toward.

Perhaps Robin will race again, perhaps not. But in a very real way he helps us define the road to renewal, because after every exhausting racing experience he has to begin all over again. From his story we learn about faith and perseverance. We are inspired. We are challenged. And, of course, we are renewed.

STEVE DUNN

Chapter Seven

"The highest reward for a person's toil is not what they get for it, but what they become by it."
JOHN RUSKIN

THE CROWDER PEA PRINCIPLE

We are blessed with a wonderfully functional and attractive cafeteria at Alexis PlaySafe. It provides a warm and friendly environment for lunch and conversation. Through the years, however, the food selections haven't always measured up to the same standard. For too long, the choices were a stale salad bar, vending machines, or bringing lunch from home. Going out to a restaurant usually takes too long and can be too expensive, so many of us had no workable alternative at lunchtime.

I've always been a proponent of good hot food for lunch, so the cafeteria situation was something that gnawed at me for years. That is, until we met Steve Dunn, owner of Jake's restaurant in our hometown of Gainesville, Georgia.

Long before Steve bought Jake's, the restaurant enjoyed a good reputation for serving hearty breakfasts and delicious hot lunches. Then, a few years ago, that changed. People stopped going to Jake's so much. So did I. The food was okay but not exceptional, and the atmosphere was dull and lifeless. With each visit I couldn't help noticing that there were more and more empty parking spaces.

Then Steve bought the restaurant and within six months he accomplished a remarkable turnaround. Today, Jake's is one of Gainesville's most popular restaurants for quality southern cooking. The food and the service are excellent and the parking lot stays full. Satisfied customers are everywhere. If ever there was a story of renewal, in a business sense, Jake's is it.

The remarkable turnaround at Jake's didn't go unnoticed by us. Sometime after meeting him at the restaurant, we invited him to speak to our "Rethink Group" about the secrets of his success. Out of that experience an idea emerged. Since many of our employees enjoyed the food at Jake's, and since we are blessed with a sizable cafeteria, we asked Steve if he would help us out of our lunchtime dilemma. He agreed, and today there's a "Jake's at Featherbone," serving delicious hot breakfast and lunch, ably managed by Jeff Coker, a very pleasant and agreeable protégé of Steve's.

While the food remains the most obvious benefit of this

Jeff Coker

new arrangement, Jake's at Featherbone has given us much more than nutrition for the body. There has been a surprising renewal in another sense. Call it food for the soul. To understand that, you need to know a little more about Steve Dunn, the people who work for him, and the principles that have guided him to success in the food service business.

A lot of his success can be attributed to his attitude about service. Owning a restaurant is a tough business, but Steve Dunn knows what it takes to keep customers coming back. One story about just how far Steve will go to satisfy his customers is almost legendary. It goes like this.

One day a regular customer at Jake's came in and posed a question to Steve: 'You have had every kind of pea I can think of, but what about crowder peas?' So Steve searched the markets and the next time the man came in, Steve told him he had found some. The man said, 'Oh yeah, when are you going to serve them?' Steve asked him when he would be coming back, and the two agreed on a day. The man returned and had his crowder peas.

Searching the markets for a particular kind of pea may seem like a whole lot of effort just to make one customer happy. And it is. But in the food service business, a restaurant owner has to be willing to cater to individual taste. Steve takes that willingness a step further. He's eager about it, to the point that new customers are surprised and old ones remain loyal. Steve Dunn refers to it as the "Crowder Pea Principle," which means that you offer a variety of food and you are flexible in your products. It means you give customers what they want so they will come back.

The Crowder Pea Principle is but one principle among many that Steve applies in his business. He calls them "Secrets of Jake's Success." As a longtime veteran of the food service industry, he didn't learn them overnight. He began his career in food service in the '80s as a grill cook with the Wendy's fast-food chain. His work ethic quickly got him noticed, and within a few weeks he was promoted to manager.

"Wendy's gave me an opportunity to be as successful as I wanted to be," Steve says. "Whatever effort I put into it, that's what I got out of it. I knew I could be like a lot of managers who were on their way out, or I could get in there, hustle, and help the company grow." Steve chose the latter, and for seven years he worked as a manager at a number of Wendy's locations. Because his attitude and work ethic were so infectious, and because he was single and mobile, Steve became the manager that Wendy's turned to for help in turning around distressed stores. In each situation he made the store successful because he worked as if the company were his own. As much as anyone in the organization, he was helping to build the Wendy's brand...at the same time developing a lifelong network of friends in food business. During that time, he learned all he could about restaurant management, including Wendy's three-pronged approach, or "QSC."

"QSC stands for quality, service and cleanliness...and in that order," Steve explains. "You start with quality, because you can have the best service in the world and a clean environment, but if the food is poor quality, none of that matters. A friend in the business once told me you could have a restaurant in the middle of a toxic waste dump if you serve good food."

In the restaurant business, as in any other, building a brand is important. Branding is the art of creating a community of people who staunchly believe in the brand and what it stands for. Harley riders, for example, wouldn't be caught dead on a Kawasaki, and nine out of ten wear Levi's blue jeans… and only Levi's. Wendy's created a community that attracted Steve. He believed in what they stood for, and today he has created his own circle of faithful customers at Jake's.

"It is definitely a community at Jake's," Steve says. "There are certain groups of people who come in not only for the food but also for the fellowship. They know they can sit and eat, drink coffee, and talk with other people. Some of our elderly, retired customers come in for breakfast every morning just because they want to talk to the employees and other customers. We have created a very real community here at

Jake's for them."

Steve's knack for making customers feel at home starts with his employees. His leadership style serves as a great model for those of us who bear that responsibility. Again, the underlying principles come from his past experience.

After his years at Wendy's, Steve eventually took on a manager role at Curt's Cafeteria, a restaurant located in Oakwood, Georgia, a few miles south of Gainesville. The restaurant was struggling to make money and the owner was moving the business to a larger location. An effective manager was needed. Once again Steve brought his talents to the situation and helped to turn it around. By pitching in on any and all menial tasks, and paying particular attention to the wishes of each customer, Steve modeled a new level of customer service for his employees. Within a month, he doubled the breakfast business. Within a few months after that, the rest of the business took off, and Curt's became another Steve Dunn turnaround success story.

For seven more years Steve managed Curt's and continued to grow the business for the owner. But as he approached his fortieth birthday, he began to experience a nagging feeling that it was time to build yet another successful restaurant business – only this time his own.

"I always wanted a place of my own," Steve recalls, "so with the help of a good friend in the food business, I identified three possibilities in the Gainesville area. Jake's was one of them."

In its early years, Jake's had been successful. It was in a good location and the owners were personable and good managers. But in time the business declined. Age and health problems led the owners to consider selling and getting out of the business. Enter Steve Dunn, who saw nothing but opportunity. He bought the business and set about doing what he knew best.

"My number one priority," recalls Steve, "was to give the place a facelift. I wanted people to walk in the door and say, 'Wow, this place is different.' So I changed the wallpaper, painted, and put marble in the vestibule. Then, I changed to a self-serve line, because I had heard from customers even before I bought the place that the servings were too small. So I let people serve themselves, which some people argue doesn't work. But over time, I've seen that it does."

As important as those changes were, Steve says that the big difference between the old Jake's and the new was the quality of the food. Even if he paid more for his ingredients, he was determined to provide the best quality food for his customers. To improve the breakfast quality, he bought the best bacon he could find and offered patrons biscuits made from scratch. For lunch and dinner, he bought real cubed steak instead of processed patties. He opted for fresh chicken tenders instead of frozen, and real potatoes instead of instant. All through his daily menu, he gave his cook (the same cook who had worked there previously) the license to prepare quality dishes using quality ingredients. The cook eagerly rose to meet the challenge and immediately the quality of the food improved. And, of course, his customers loved it.

While the food was the primary attraction for his early customers, enthusiastic service-oriented employees were also a draw. At Jake's, Steve had begun operation with a crew that was completely new to him. Some of the employees at Curt's had indicated a willingness to follow him to Jake's, but Steve was careful not to "steal" employees away from his former employer. A man of principle, he was clear on that subject. He also chose to remain closed on Sundays, one of the most lucrative days of the week for restaurants. He found, however, that the new business from Jake's at Featherbone and his other loyal customers gave him enough business during the week that closing on Sunday was not a problem.

Granny Lou

"Granny Lou" Westmoreland, born in Gainesville, Georgia, into a family of 14 children, was raised on a farm by parents she adored. Her first job off the farm was in a hosiery mill. She later went to Chicopee Mills and retired from its successor, Johnson & Johnson, after 36 years of service. Granny Lou met Steve Dunn in 1984. The two adopted each other and have worked together ever since. Today, at age 86, Granny Lou is famous in North Georgia for her legendary baking at Jake's.

Along the way, Granny has suffered life's heartbreaks, which include the death of her beloved husband and son. In addition, at age 54, Granny Lou experienced severe back problems and was told by her doctor that she would thereafter be an invalid, never to walk or work again. For a while she didn't walk or work and, in fact, cleaned her home on her hands and knees. Then she decided things would be different. She got up, returned to work and hasn't looked back since.

Her advice to anyone who is going through tough times:

1.   You don't know what you can do until you actually try it. She admonished her doctors to never tell anyone they can't work.

2.   Have faith in God and know that prayers will be answered for the things we truly need.

3.   God can handle our problems when we can't. Turn them over to Him. "And don't go back to get 'em!"

Granny leaves this thought of renewal with the people she meets: "God loves you and I love you, too."

That's good enough for me.

At our company Steve has established yet another community, not too different from the way a church establishes a mission. We are renewed by the professionalism and genuine, caring attitude of both Steve and Jeff Coker. The food renews us physically, but the community they have helped us establish there renews us in a spiritual sense.

Steve Dunn is a master at bringing renewal to restaurants in decline, but he is also a master at bringing renewal to those he meets. Included in his "Five Secrets of Jake's Success" is the notion that success comes when you base your business on principles that come before business. That's often much easier said than done. Steve Dunn, however, makes it look easy.

THE JACK DANIEL'S "CREATING COMMUNITY" TEAM:
STANDING LEFT TO RIGHT, JAY HANAUER, JIM MASSEY;
SEATED LEFT TO RIGHT, CHRIS MORRIS, JIM CHILDS, BILL COLEMAN

Chapter Eight

*"Talent does what it can.
Genius does what it must."*
UNKNOWN

JACK DANIEL'S
"CREATING COMMUNITY"
BRANDING CONFERENCE

In the last chapter we have seen renewal brought to our company by the individuals of a "supplier" business located very near us. In a real way they have become a vital part of our supply chain. Over the years many great customers and suppliers have renewed us. No better example exists, however, than our partnership with retail leader Dillard Department Stores and textile innovator Milliken & Company. Working with the talented people of both organizations our company has been regularly renewed in the areas of business strategy, product research and development, design, marketing, advertising, consumer research, information systems, and logistics. And, because of that renewal, all have prospered.

But what about corporate renewal being brought to us by a company that has no direct interest in our business? Is that really possible? How can such a company bring renewal? In this chapter you'll discover what we did. It is about community, authenticity and validation. And this lesson interestingly comes from Lynchburg, Tennessee.

According to Business Week magazine, Jack Daniel's is one of the top 100 brands in the world. Defined in these terms: "Flamboyantly down-home antimarketing approach endears the Tennessee sippin' whiskey to an expanding band of loyalists," Jack Daniel's is well ahead of everyone else in their field. Number two is not even close. The value of the brand name alone is two billion dollars.

In a way, the appeal of Jack Daniel's has more to do with its authenticity and down-home values than it does with whiskey. The Jack Daniel's people have created a worldwide family who believe in these values as they do. And from that has come the phenomenon of Jack Daniel's and billions of dollars in sales from many, many Jack Daniel's products ranging from the Tennessee sippin' whiskey itself to apparel and housewares.

If you'd like a CD of music by the Silver Cornet Band, drop us a line.

JACK DANIEL'S SILVER CORNET BAND
WAS STARTED BY JACK DANIEL HIMSELF. BUT IT TOOK A WHILE TO CATCH ON.

May this be your day
To plow straight behind a willing mule
To whittle a tight curl
And to pitch nothing but ringers
Without hardly trying

JACK DANIEL'S TOAST

In the summer of 2001, I was invited to speak before the Jack Daniel's company at their annual conference in Tucson, Arizona. What an unusual opportunity! What could I share with such a totally different company from ours that would have value to them? Somehow, in discussing our company's journey through the years, a connection was made. Less than a year later it would bring us together in Gainesville.

We invited Jay Hanauer, president of the Brown-Forman Distillery Company and producer of Jack Daniel's, to visit with us at Alexis PlaySafe for a "Creating Community" Branding Conference. The idea behind the Branding Conference was for all of us to better understand branding. In addition, we hoped to view Alexis PlaySafe, Inc. from the perspective of a completely different organization. Not only did he accept our invitation, he brought with him a wonderfully gifted team of creative thinkers: Bill Coleman, President,

Brown-Forman Cooperages; Jim Chiles, SVP Technology and Development; Jim Massey, Director of Human Resources; and Chris Morris, Master Distiller (in training) and Director of Marketing Excellence. These individuals had experience in the Jack Daniel's business as well as backgrounds in other Brown-Forman Companies including Hartmann Luggage, Lenox China, Gorham Silver, Dansk tableware, and other well-known consumer brands. Also invited to the conference were Leonard Brewington and Jerry Marella, representatives of our largest supplier, Milliken & Co., and Tracy Vardeman, head of strategic planning for our healthcare provider, Northeast Georgia Medical Center. The backgrounds of the attendees were varied and the potential for creative thinking was powerful.

In April 2002 we met for two days. The agenda: On Day One we heard the Alexis PlaySafe brand stories and strategic plans. On Day Two, the Jack Daniel's team assumed the role of "new owners" of our company and shared their observations with the group. It was a meeting we would never forget. It brought us renewal...through rediscovery (in the business sense) of our authentic self.

In preparation for the conference, Tracy Vardeman inspired us to read the book, *Movies To Manage By*, specifically the chapter on *Hoosiers* starring Gene Hackman. Everyone read that assignment and watched the videotape of the movie before coming to the meeting. That provided the perfect backdrop to begin our discussions of branding. The movie dealt with the building of a State Champion high school basketball team through the unconventional efforts of Coach Norman Dale. What became apparent to us is that leaders, like Coach Dale, create community. That community is built on authentic internalized values that speak to more than just the sport. They begin the process as healers by caring about relationship issues that hinder performance in their players. In this sense they develop teams, which become "brands" in their communities. Their "brand" inspires those within the community as well as the many outside who want to get in.

The Alexis PlaySafe team then presented its business plans for all three company divisions, Alexis (newborn baby apparel), PlaySafe (flotation swimsuits and accessories), and Private Label branding. These plans included the business purpose and vision, sales volumes and trends, demographic analyses, sourcing, and marketing strategies. By the end of Day One our guests had been provided all there was to know about our businesses. Or at least we thought so!

Throughout the discussions it became clear to all of us that brands must be internally consistent to be externally believable. We have to live what we say we believe. The outward reflection of those beliefs over time creates the brand. The brand then becomes an attractor to others who want to join the community. Further, as noted by Scott Bedbury in his book, *A New Brand World – Eight Principles for Achieving Brand Leadership in the 21st Century*, one must "attach the brand to a higher principle, which connects to the core business; yet provides emotional benefits that transcend the physical ones." Other notable brand communities that demonstrate that connection are Saturn, Harley Davidson and John Deere.

Next, the Jack Daniel's group assumed their role as "new owners" of our company and told us what they saw in us...who they thought we were at the core. All on the basis of one day's exposure to us! Sometimes it just doesn't take much time if the observer is truly interested in the subject.

Among the weaknesses the new owners found: not enough brand development, reliance on the distribution network (stores) for sales, not enough consumer "pull" (consequence of underdeveloped brands), rapidly changing retail distribution network, and relatively high production costs.

Having said that, the "new owners" went on to say that the really important raw materials for leadership and brand building actually existed. We had going for us:

- ***100% USA credentials***
- ***Authentic and sustainable heritage***
- ***Loyal employee support (Average tenure in our company is nine years.)***

- **PROXIMITY TO AN INTERNATIONAL CITY (ATLANTA)**
- **SMALL PRODUCTION LOT CAPABILITY/EXPERTISE**
- **AN EXPANDING CONSUMER BASE**
- **SOUTHERN CHARM!**

They even suggested a descriptor for the Alexis PlaySafe company:

"Real People - Real Families - Real Caring."

With these assets at hand, and with smart marketing (guerrilla and otherwise), we had a foundation for looking to the future. That is the renewal brought to us that day. And we'll never forget it.

Our meeting with Jack Daniel's illustrates how renewal often happens in an organization. They helped us rediscover real assets easily overlooked. It was about not "throwing out the baby with the bathwater." It was about getting back down to our essence. Because of their validation, we began appreciating anew what we had begun to take for granted. In a way it's like refinishing furniture. First, remove all those layers of paint/finish until you uncover the beauty of the natural wood. See the genius (in your genes) and build from there.

Throughout the ages philosophers have reminded mankind of this truth. A carved Greek inscription from 600

BC says "KNOW THYSELF." Shakespeare, in the sixteenth century, said, "This above all: to thine own self be true, and it must follow, as the night the day, Thou canst not then be false to any man." Psychologist Dr. Phil McGraw, brought to public prominence today by Oprah Winfrey, has made in-your-face straight talk almost an art form. One of the greatest needs he sees in people is that of really knowing themselves. He maintains that many of us don't and, as a consequence, we wind up frustrated in trying to live someone else's life.

As we are renewed by others, we find our real selves. Our brand. The dictionary says that a brand is a "kind, grade or make as indicated by a stamp, trademark, or the like." And just like the branding principles discovered in the Jack Daniel's example, we must be internally consistent to be externally believable. In our role as leaders and builders of our brand we create a community that attracts others by the values it represents.

So, reader, what is your brand - your trademark? How will people know you have traveled this way? What do you leave behind in the people you have touched? Does the authentic in you speak to the authentic in them? One of the greatest gifts we present to this world is the gift of renewal we bring to others by validating what's real in them. Arguably, it's why we are here.

Jese McElveen and Lamar Morse, best friends for seventy years.

Chapter Nine

> *"The entire sum of existence is the magic of
> being needed by just one person."*
> Vi Putnam

It Starts with Two

Renewal connects us with each other and ourselves. Absence of that connection can be seen in many places. The costs of personal disconnect are enormous.

Christmas holidays, for instance, are difficult for many people. It is easy for the "hype of the holidays" to bring on despair, loneliness, separation, and unfulfilled expectations. In extreme cases the disease of depression can bring on suicide. Suicides, in fact, significantly increase between Christmas and New Year.

According to the CDC in Atlanta, suicides have grown to be the 11th leading cause of death among all Americans and the third leading cause of death among young people 15-24. For the young, suicide claims more lives than heart disease, cancer, AIDS, birth defects, stroke, and chronic lung disease combined. Males are four times more likely to die from suicide than females. Among males, white males are substantially more likely to die from suicide than blacks.

Suicide rates increase with age. Risk factors include illness, depression, and isolation. Considering isolation, it is interesting to note that the lowest incidence of suicide is in New York/New Jersey and the highest in the western states like Nevada.

Personal connection and renewal are critical for living. Renewal connects us to ourselves and to each other. In the process we become less isolated, less depressed and more hopeful. And that outlook of hope makes all the difference. Just ask Dr. Dale Anderson who maintains that happiness and laughter, especially when it is shared with others, are learned skills that enhance well-being and longevity.

Dr. Dale Anderson is a Minneapolis-based physician with over 40 years experience. He has practiced as a family doctor, a board-certified Mayo Clinic trained general surgeon, and a board-certified emergency physician. He is part of the Urgent Care Medicine Department of Park Nicollet Clinic, one of the country's largest multi-specialty clinics. Dr. Anderson also holds certification as a Diplomate of the American Board of Holistic Medicine.

In addition, he is well known as a prolific writer and speak-

DR. DALE ANDERSON

er on the benefits of smiling and laughing, and how it results in a psychological bond that dramatically benefits health. On the subject of connection, I asked him to share his thoughts with us.

"I believe that it is impossible for human beings to enjoy optimum health unless they experience genuine connection. Here I use the word "connection" in its broadest sense - bonding with friends, family, lovers, nature and community.

At its most basic and primal level, connection means touch. Research with both animals and humans shows the debilitating effects that can occur when touching ceases to be a part of our lives. We fail to thrive physically and emotionally; we become more insecure and prone to illness. Further difficulties arise when we associate touching exclusively with sex. This is a hang-up in our society, in which people are generally touch-starved due to sexual taboos.

We can overcome this problem in small yet significant ways. A simple handshake, or a smile or laugh, has the power to bond people in ways that are non-threatening. So when touching is ATT (appropriate, timely and tasteful) and when mutually acceptable, give the pat on the shoulder and everyday gestures of friendliness and support.

Of course there are other ways to foster connection than physical touch. One way is to spend non-hurried time with colleagues and friends. People appreciate being asked about their homes, families, travel plans and reactions to a meeting. So much of customer service boils down to the simple act of asking questions, listening to answers, and responding appropriately.

When we talk about the "chemistry" of a life acted well, we're discussing something literal. Memorable relationships are those where one feels a strong and lasting sense of being included...and they're memorable because they are endorphin raisers. (Note: endorphins and other "emotional" chemistries are produced naturally by our bodies and induce feelings of pleasure and well-being.) *These feelings of belonging and camaraderie perpetuate the chemistry of happiness."*

This book has talked about the connection and renewal that only we can bring to each other. How do we begin? By recognizing the need, of course...for others and ourselves. Then, by reaching out for the connections with no preconceived notions of the outcome. We're not in control of that...thank God!

Will we remember what we have learned from the example of 60-year old Dien Do and what he taught all of us about patriotism as he climbed that flagpole? Will we also remember that we, like Ole, can have a profound positive effect on the life of another...at exactly the right time?

How have we been renewed by Dave Sloyer's life? Will we remember that it is the journey, not the destination? Will we ever look at the sea and not remember Robin Davie who, after sailing around the world alone three different times, warns us that the most treacherous seas are the calm seas?

Have we been touched by the simplicity and elegance of the "secrets of Jakes" that apply to any business organization? And finally, are we authentic as defined by the Jack Daniel's story? Does the authentic in us connect with the authentic in others?

As we renew others and are renewed by them, we are set to grow again, day after day, regardless of our age. As a result, the possibilities of our personal springtimes are endless. The more we renew, the more we are renewed.

All the people in this book have walked into my life, unannounced; but they have changed forever the way I look at life. Do you and I live expectantly, looking for the renewal that's offered by the "angels among us"? Start looking for them. You'll find them in ordinary places.

Recently my wife, Nell, and I went out to lunch after church. I had not been to that particular restaurant in well over a year. On our arrival, Linda, the food and beverage manager, greeted us warmly just as she had about a year before.

My mind raced back to that winter visit during an ice storm that paralyzed Gainesville and cut off power to many homes, ours included. No power, no heat, no hot coffee and food. No good. So we got in the car and drove to town. Most places were closed of course. I noticed that the Waffle House was open. 200 cars seemed jammed into their lot built for 20. Standing room only inside. We drove on... and found that the Holiday Inn was also somehow open. We went into the restaurant and found an unforgettable sight: smiling Linda, who had left her family at home to come to work, and an unbelievably beautiful buffet with lots of hot coffee. Others came later, but for a long time it was just the three of us. A communion of sorts. Each person grateful for the other.

As Nell and I approached Linda this time I wondered if she would remember that bond formed a year ago. She did. But in an instant I sensed great pain beneath her smile. Hesitating to speak at first, she then said, "I lost my daughter in a car accident this July. We don't know exactly what happened...but I want you to know. Somehow that helps."

Who was renewed? In that brief encounter Linda helped me connect...to the authentic human being in me who, like her, understands what it means to lose someone. Perhaps I helped her, too, in knowing that her loss was now shared by at least one other who cared. In that moment each was validated and, in the process, renewed. The holiday season was just a few weeks away. Just possibly this brief instance of renewal would help each of us find a greater meaning in the season. And then somehow help others.

We bring renewal to each other. It's a very simple principle. It's life changing and life sustaining.

It starts with two.

Epilogue

Dear reader:

Before you go I want to share one more example of renewal...this time of an entire industry that is critical to our way of life. That industry is manufacturing. The people who are renewing it are our young people. There is hope.

GUS WHALEN
GAINESVILLE, GA
SPRING 2003

HOPE IN THE GREEN BUD

"We call it spring, and we celebrate it as Easter and as Passover. It is renewal, rebirth, release from the winter of the soul. It is faith and belief triumphant. And it is written in so simple a place as the bursting bud."

HAL BORLAND

In the fall of 2002, the United States endured a prolonged West Coast dockworkers strike. For several weeks, shipments of manufactured products from abroad came to a stop. Nothing moved. We all waited for merchandise that is no longer made in the United States. Some claimed that the late display of Christmas decorations at Wal-Mart that year was caused by the strike. Whatever the truth, we all received a vivid reminder that the US manufacturing base mentioned in Chapter 1 has increasingly moved offshore. That manufacturing output, often of essential products, floated on thousands of containers awaiting entry into the USA. Am I suggesting that our country is at risk (beyond delaying Christmas) as we lose our manufacturing base? Yes I am.

It is my belief that manufacturing is one of the three primary ways any country creates wealth, along with agriculture and mining/drilling. As we increase imports we transfer vital manufacturing expertise to lands far away. So our appetite for consumption has grown but our ability to produce for that consumption has seriously declined. And further, in an age of terrorism, I believe that manufacturing is at the core of what we should now think of as Homeland Security. It is winter for manufacturing; but spring is coming.

We began our journey together through this book with a story about the renewal of a company that has a long heritage in several fields, especially manufacturing. Our journey closes for now with a quiet groundbreaking in 2002 for a new technical high school in Worcester, Massachusetts. That school represents a bursting bud for manufacturing, with "faith and belief triumphant." It signals a growing awareness of the critical importance of young people who have the advanced technical education to make things. Those things help feed, clothe, house, transport and protect us. That groundbreaking did not make the national news as did the dockworkers strike. But the school that will emerge, with its graduates, and those that follow in every state, will very likely transform our nation's future. Here's the story.

The center of the Industrial Revolution in the United States and the manufacturing that resulted was in the

Northeast, especially Massachusetts. Worcester, MA, also became a center for the tool and die industry. That industry creates the machines that are then used in manufacturing. Worcester was both a technology center and also the home to industrial education with the creation of this nation's first vocational school in 1908. The school opened with 50 male students, half in woodworking and half in ironworking. The cost to establish the school was about $150,000.

Originally the school was not part of the public school system and was operated by an independent board of trustees. Many saw the need for a girl's trade school and one was opened in 1911. It later burned and was replaced largely through a gift in 1917 of $100,000 by the Royal Worcester Corset Company that employed 1000 stitchers in the area. At that time our company manufactured patented Warren's Featherbone, a stiffening material sewn into corsets. So very likely our company had at least an indirect connection to vocational education in Worcester. Also in 1917, what is now the Warren Featherbone Foundation was formed.

Ironically, 85 years later in October 2002, (during that dock strike) I would represent the Warren Featherbone Foundation in making a Warren Featherbone Foundation award to Worcester's "New" Vocational High School and its leadership. The award was made in partnership with Tony Smith and Tec, Inc., and was presented to Peter Crafts,

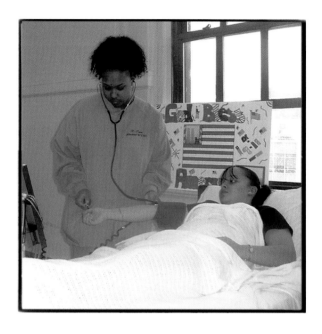

Director for the Vocational Department of the Worcester Public Schools; Jack Healy, Director of Mass Manufacturing Extension Partnership; Mike Hogan, President of Mass Development; and Ted Coughlin, Chair of Advisory Boards.

Upon completion, Worcester's Vocational High School will likely be the largest vocational high school ever built. Covering 400,000 square feet, the school will accommodate 4500 students between day and night programs. Four academies are being created within the school (Construction, Manufacturing, Health, and Business) covering twenty-four

disciplines. Both academic and vocational programs are being integrated to provide a balanced education. Peter Crafts, Director of Vocational/Technical Education explains:

"Students encounter 'real life' experiences through exposure to practical, work-related situations and problems. Strong emphasis will be placed on developing problem-solving skills, interpersonal skills, and the ability to work in teams; and on professional competencies including responsibility, sociability, self-management, integrity, and honesty."

The citizens of Worcester and Massachusetts are investing an incredible 90 million dollars into this project and have created a nine-to-one match for all donations to the school. The Worcester Vocational High School phenomenon represents a significant shift nationally. Technical and career education is growing rapidly across the country because it speaks so clearly to the needs of our students and our country.

The city of Worcester is also experiencing "urban renewal" as the new Vocational High School is being constructed on the sight of a former state hospital that backs up to the gorgeous 500-acre Green Park which rises above the city.

The award ceremony for Worcester's Vocational High School was held during Massachusetts' Manufacturing Week, proclaimed by Governor Jane Swift. Our foundation has been active in promoting state manufacturing weeks beginning with our co-founding of the 1995 celebration in Georgia. During that important first year Nancy Flanagan, our company's purchasing agent, provided valuable leadership within our company. The foundation was then in place for expansion into other states. Today several states officially sponsor manufacturing appreciation weeks in addition to Georgia. We have participated in celebrations in Delaware, South Carolina, Massachusetts, and Maine, and our objective is for all 50 states to become involved. The purpose of these weeks is to raise awareness of the importance of manufacturing to our economy and careers in manufacturing for our young people.

2003 will begin the 10th anniversary year of Manufacturing Appreciation Week in Georgia. This event will also launch a joint effort to take the manufacturing message nationwide. The Georgia Department of Technical and Adult Education under the leadership of Dr. Ken Breeden, Jackie Rohosky, and their talented associates in 34 technical colleges in Georgia have played a vital role in the success of this initiative in the state and beyond. Vocational education is the key to world-class manufacturing. Accordingly, technical schools across the country are forming the base from which our country can and must be reindustrialized.

Most importantly, education meets the needs of young people. And, of course, young people in all careers are our future. They renew us, reminding us often of who we were before "experience" and the years changed us. In our company today you will see a quotation that speaks to all of us. It reminds us of a truth and implies an obligation.

> *"Children are living messages*
> *we send to a time we will not see."*
>
> — UNKNOWN

I often work with grandparents. They would quickly agree, as Hal Borland observed about spring, that children "provide renewal, rebirth, release from the winter of the soul."

Our obligation is to invest ourselves and our resources into children. They not only renew us. They also provide our legacy to the future.

Hope in the green bud.

About the Author

Charles E. "Gus" Whalen, Jr. is Chairman and Chief Executive Officer of Alexis PlaySafe, Inc. and the Warren Featherbone Company in Gainesville, Georgia. In 1993, he re-established the Warren Featherbone Foundation, originally founded in 1917, to increase public awareness of the importance of interdependent connections in business and throughout society. His first two books, *The Featherbone Principle: A Declaration of Interdependence*, and *The Featherbone Spirit: Celebrating Life's Connections*, have reached a wide audience and continue to be distributed through the Foundation and Amazon.com.

Acknowledgements

I have learned that books, like most worthwhile endeavors, require the talents of many people. This book has been blessed in attracting some wonderfully gifted individuals who have put a little of themselves in these pages. I want you to know them....

Phil Bellury – *Phil is my co-author and collaborator of four books, a videotape and numerous other projects. He is my friend and always-wise counselor.*

Laurie Shock – *Strictly speaking, Laurie is the very talented designer of this book and her work speaks for itself. Laurie is much more though. Her contributions to my understanding of renewal unlocked many doors.*

Billy Howard – *Most of the photography in this book is the work of a very well known photographer, Billy Howard. Besides technical skill, Billy has a great heart for this book's central message—majesty resides in all people. You can see it in their faces.*

The "heavy lifting" in producing a book comes in the numerous rewrites. The editing function for this book has been greatly facilitated by these individuals who spent a great deal of time in reading and making suggestions for the final manuscript.

Dr. Dale Anderson – *Park Nicollet Clinic – Minneapolis, Minnesota*

Susan Black – *VNU Business Publications USA – Columbia, South Carolina*

Dr. Ken Breeden – *Georgia Department of Technical and Adult Education– Atlanta, Georgia*

Phil Condit – *The Boeing Company – Chicago, Illinois*

Dr. Bill Coates – *First Baptist Church – Gainesville, Georgia*

Robin Davie – *Sail South Carolina – Charleston, South Carolina*

Steve Dunn – *Jake's – Gainesville, Georgia*

Chris Cosper, Evelyn Dunagan, Nancy Flanagan, Kathryn Smith and **Doris Whalen** – *Alexis PlaySafe, Inc. – Gainesville, Georgia*

Ed Emma – *Jockey International, Inc. – Kenosha, Wisconsin*

Bill Holder – *Dillard Department Stores – Little Rock, Arkansas*

Jay Hanauer and **Bill Coleman** – *Brown-Forman Company – Louisville, Kentucky*

Lee Lathrop – *Retired, The Boeing Company – Toledo, Washington*

James Mathis – *Retired, Trust Company Bank of North Georgia – Gainesville, Georgia*

Jim Mathis – *North Georgia Community Foundation – Gainesville, Georgia*

W.H. (Dink) Nesmith – *Community Newspapers, Inc. – Athens, Georgia*

Sam Oliver, *Attorney – Gainesville, Georgia*

Ed Primeau – *Primeau Productions – Southfield, Michigan*

Linda Robertson – *Holiday Inn – Gainesville, Georgia*

Dr. Bill Self – *John's Creek Baptist Church – Duluth, Georgia*

Wes Sarginson – *WXIA TV – Atlanta, Georgia*

David Sloyer – *Sarchi Foods – Cleveland, Georgia*

Mary Ann Whalen – *our daughter and genetic counselor – Greenville, South Carolina*

Eddie Whalen – *our son and composer – Atlanta, Georgia*

Your Order Form
for staying connected!

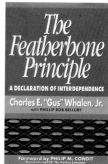

No matter who you are, your life is made richer through your connection with the people in your family, your workplace and community. These three richly illustrated books, with their positive message of recognizing the value of our "connectedness" make excellent gifts for those you care about.

And remember, it's for a good cause. These books are published by The Warren Featherbone Foundation, whose mission is to raise awareness of the importance of interdependent connections in business and in our personal lives. Be sure you have the entire set!

Just Published! The Gift of Renewal   Qty. _____ @ $19.95 ea = $ _____

The Featherbone Spirit   Qty. _____ @ $19.95 ea = $ _____

The Featherbone Principle   Qty. _____ @ $19.95 ea = $ _____

Add $4.00 <u>each</u> for shipping and handling = $ _____
(On orders of 10 or more books there are no shipping and handling fees)

Total = $ _____

Name _____

Shipping address _____

City _____ State _____ ZIP _____

Phone _____ Credit card type ☐ Mastercard ☐ Visa

Credit card no. _____ Exp. date _____

Signature _____

Fill out above information, include payment, and send to:
The Warren Featherbone Foundation, P.O. Box 383, Gainesville, GA 30503